MATHEMATICS ON THE MOVE

CONTENTS

JAMES BURNETT
CALVIN IRONS

LAND, AIR, SEA

People have always traveled – to search for food and water, to trade with other people, or to explore foreign lands. Over the centuries, many forms of transport have been developed to make travel as fast and convenient as possible. People have also developed some forms of transport that are used mostly for fun.

On the Rails

The first regular passenger rail service opened in England in 1830. It used steam locomotives that had a top speed of 29 miles per hour. Today's high-speed electric trains can reach speeds of more than 300 miles per hour.

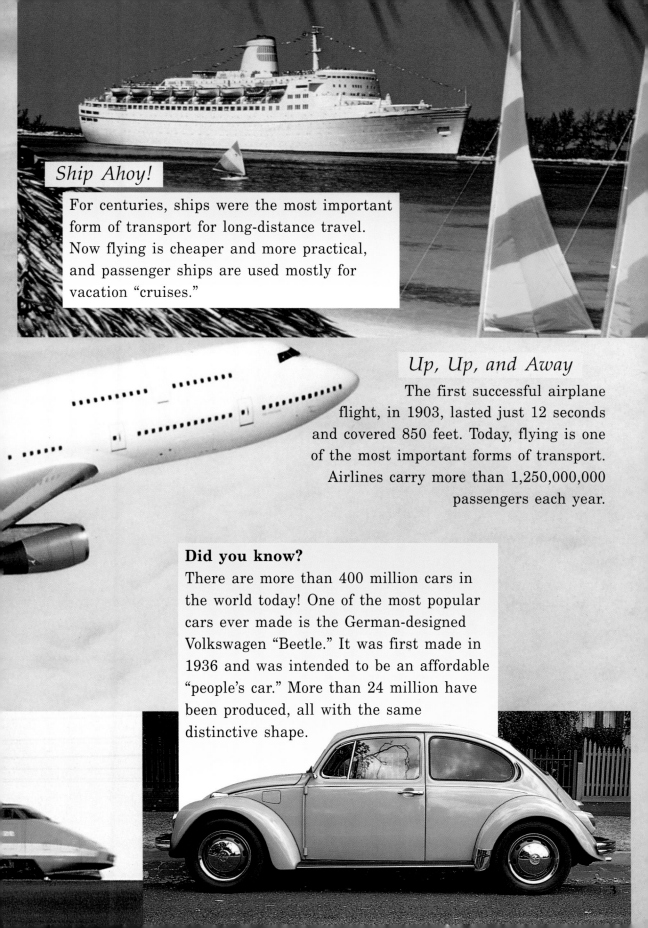

Ship Ahoy!

For centuries, ships were the most important form of transport for long-distance travel. Now flying is cheaper and more practical, and passenger ships are used mostly for vacation "cruises."

Up, Up, and Away

The first successful airplane flight, in 1903, lasted just 12 seconds and covered 850 feet. Today, flying is one of the most important forms of transport. Airlines carry more than 1,250,000,000 passengers each year.

Did you know?

There are more than 400 million cars in the world today! One of the most popular cars ever made is the German-designed Volkswagen "Beetle." It was first made in 1936 and was intended to be an affordable "people's car." More than 24 million have been produced, all with the same distinctive shape.

3

MOVING RIGHT ALONG

There are many different ways of moving people around. Some forms of transport are much faster than others.

Distance traveled in 10 minutes at a safe speed

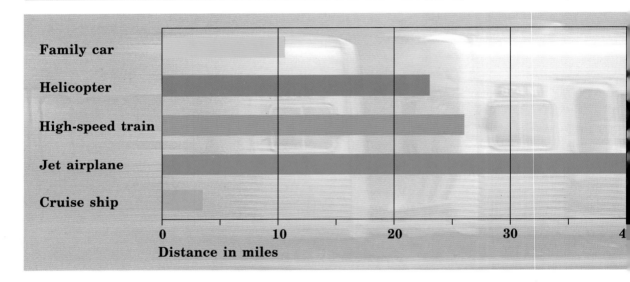

esearch

- List some different forms of transport you could use to travel to your closest major city.

  Find out the costs and traveling times for the different forms of transport.

  Which form of transport would you choose? Why?

The bar graph and the chart both provide the same information.

Vehicle	Distance traveled in 10 minutes at a safe speed
Family car	$10\frac{1}{2}$ miles
Helicopter	23 miles
High-speed train	26 miles
Jet airplane	93 miles
Cruise ship	$3\frac{1}{2}$ miles

Use the graph and/or the chart to help you answer questions 1, 2, and 3. Write whether you used the chart or the graph to answer the questions.

1. How much farther than the family car does:
   a. the helicopter travel in 10 minutes?
   b. the high-speed train travel in 10 minutes?
   c. the jet airplane travel in 10 minutes?

| 50 | 60 | 70 | 80 | 90 | 100 |

2. Which vehicle travels about twice as far as the family car in 10 minutes?

3. Write your own question about the jet plane and the high-speed train.

4. List the advantages and disadvantages of showing data:
   a. in a bar graph   b. in a chart.
   Do you think one method is better than the other? Give reasons for your answer.

MAKING TRACKS

When trains were introduced in the 1800s they quickly became the most popular form of transport, especially for long journeys. Today, many other forms of transport are available. However, trains are still important for passenger travel and for carrying many kinds of freight.

The Longest Load

In August 1989, a train measuring $4\frac{1}{2}$ miles in length traveled 535 miles in South Africa. This 76,491-ton monster, which included 16 locomotives and 660 freight cars, is the longest and heaviest freight train on record.

Railroad Networks

This chart shows the approximate distances covered by some of the world's railroad systems.

Country	Total length of track
Australia	25,000 miles
Canada	91,000 miles
China	40,000 miles
France	21,500 miles
Germany	28,100 miles
India	38,500 miles
New Zealand	2,500 miles
Russia	98,000 miles
United Kingdom	11,000 miles
United States	150,000 miles

All Aboard!

The world's longest passenger train measured 1,894 yards. This train, in Belgium, had 70 carriages, was pulled by one locomotive, and had a total weight of 3,071 tons.

Did you know?

By 1870, just 40 years after the first regular railroad service opened, the world had more than 120,000 miles of railroad track!

Never-Ending

This train transports iron ore for a mining company in Western Australia. Each ore car weighs about 26 tons and can carry a 100-ton load. The longest train ever run by the company stretched 2.4 miles in length, and had 7 diesel locomotives, and 350 ore cars.

GOING UNDER GROUND

As cities grew rapidly at the end of the 19th century, streets became more and more crowded with people and traffic. Underground railroads helped to solve this problem by allowing people to travel around below street level.

Colossal City Underground

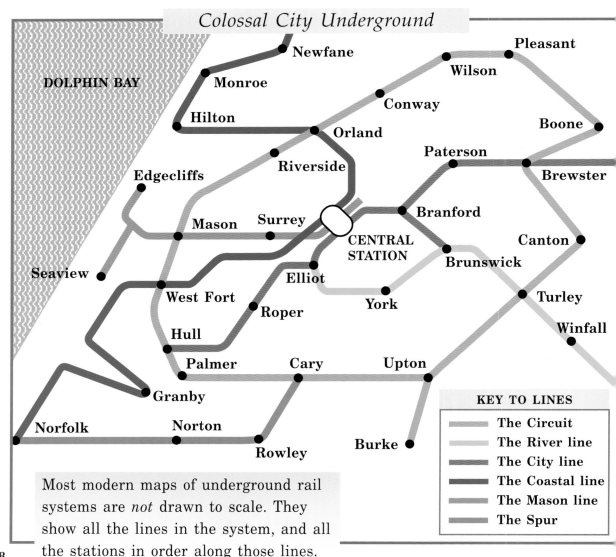

DOLPHIN BAY

Newfane

Monroe

Hilton

Edgecliffs

Mason   Surrey

Seaview

West Fort

Elliot

Roper

Hull

Palmer   Cary

Granby

Norfolk   Norton

Rowley

Riverside

Orland

Conway

Wilson

Pleasant

Boone

Paterson

Brewster

Branford

CENTRAL
STATION

Canton

Brunswick

York

Turley

Winfall

Upton

Burke

KEY TO LINES

━━━	The Circuit
━━━	The River line
━━━	The City line
━━━	The Coastal line
━━━	The Mason line
━━━	The Spur

Most modern maps of underground rail systems are *not* drawn to scale. They show all the lines in the system, and all the stations in order along those lines.

Look at the Colossal City Underground map.

1. Suppose you were traveling from Upton Station. What stations would your train go through on a trip to Norfolk?

2. Which lines connect directly with Central Station?

3. At which stations could you change from the Circuit line to:

   a. the Coastal line?   **b.** the City line?

4. List the stations you would pass, and the lines you would take, on trips from:

   a. Mason to Brunswick   **b.** Burke to Orland

   c. Winfall to Seaview.

5. Suppose you lived at Monroe. Write directions for a friend from Rowley who plans to travel by train to visit you.

MOVING THE MAIL

For thousands of years, people have sent written messages to communicate over long distances. The postal system that we use today began in the 1840s. This was when postage stamps and regular mail deliveries were introduced.

The Pony Express

In 1860, the Pony Express was established to carry mail between St. Joseph, Missouri and Sacramento, California. A team of riders covered the 1,966 miles in 10 days or less. Horses were changed at 190 "pony stations" along the route.

Australia has the longest mail route in the world. A light aircraft flies the 1,615-mile trip, across "outback" Australia, once a week.

This chart shows the approximate number of post offices in some countries. India has more post offices than *any* other country in the world.

Country	Post offices
Australia	4,400
Canada	18,500
India	150,000
New Zealand	950
United Kingdom	19,600
U.S.A.	38,000

Mountains of Mail

The U.S. Postal Service handles more than 40 percent of the world's mail. It processes about 603 million pieces of mail each day.

EXPRESS DELIVERY

People often use *express delivery* services when items need to be delivered urgently. Usually the cost depends on the weight of the package and how far it has to travel.

EXPRESS DELIVERY ZONES

A: up to 10 miles

B: up to 20 miles

C: up to 30 miles

D: up to 40 miles

E: up to 50 miles

In Colossal City, an express delivery service takes items from the city center to any area within 50 miles. The diagram and chart show the delivery zones and costs.

EXPRESS DELIVERY SERVICE					
WEIGHT CATEGORIES	**Zone A**	**Zone B**	**Zone C**	**Zone D**	**Zone E**
Up to 8 oz	1.50	1.65	1.80	1.95	2.10
Over 8 oz to 1 lb	3.00	3.30	3.60	3.90	4.20
1 lb to $1\frac{1}{2}$ lb	4.50	4.95	5.40	5.85	6.30
$1\frac{1}{2}$ lb to 2 lb	6.00	6.60	7.20	7.80	8.40
2 lb to 4 lb	6.45	7.65	8.85	10.05	11.25
4 lb to 6 lb	6.90	8.10	9.30	10.50	11.70
6 lb to 8 lb	7.35	8.55	9.75	10.95	12.15
8 lb to 10 lb	7.80	9.00	10.20	11.40	12.60
10 lb to 12 lb	8.25	9.45	10.65	11.85	13.05
12 lb to 14 lb	8.70	9.90	11.10	12.30	13.50
14 lb to 16 lb	9.15	10.35	11.55	12.75	13.95
16 lb to 18 lb	9.60	10.80	12.00	13.20	14.40
18 lb to 20 lb	10.05	11.25	12.45	13.65	14.85
20 lb to 22 lb	10.50	11.70	12.90	14.10	15.30
22 lb to 24 lb	10.95	12.15	13.35	14.55	15.75
24 lb to 26 lb	11.40	12.60	13.80	15.00	16.20
26 lb to 28 lb	11.85	13.05	14.25	15.45	16.65
28 lb to 30 lb	12.30	13.50	14.70	15.90	17.10

Look at the chart.

1. What do you notice about the weight categories:
   a. in the yellow section?   **b.** in the green section?
2. How do the costs in the green section change:
   a. *within* each zone?   **b.** *across* the zones?
3. What patterns can you find in the costs in the yellow section?
4. How much would it cost to send:
   a. a 13-lb package to an address 31 miles from the city center?
   b. a 24-lb package to an address 19 miles from the city center?
5. How much would it cost to send each of these packages from the city center?

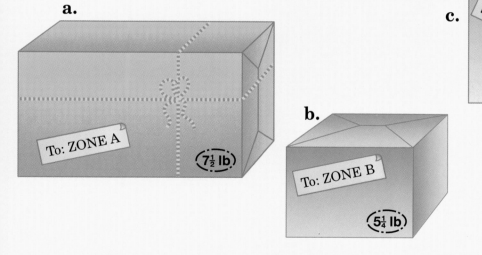

a.
To: ZONE A
$7\frac{1}{2}$ lb

b.
To: ZONE B
$5\frac{1}{4}$ lb

c.
To: ZONE C
12 lb

6. Suppose you had two 3-lb items to send to Zone E. Would you send them as two separate packages, or together as one package? Explain your decision.

PEDAL POWER

Millions of people around the world ride bicycles every day. Bicycles provide an inexpensive and non-polluting form of transport; they are also popular for exercise and leisure.

Look, No Pedals!

Some early "bicycles" did not even have pedals. The rider ran along to build up speed and then lifted his feet to enjoy the ride!

The Ordinary

The *Ordinary*, sometimes called the "penny-farthing," was first built in 1870. The pedals were attached directly to the large front wheel. Because of the size of the wheel, a single turn of the pedals moved the bicycle forward a long distance.

FRONT WHEEL
Diameter:
47 inches

Circumference:
approximately 148 inches

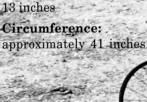

REAR WHEEL
Diameter:
13 inches

Circumference:
approximately 41 inches

By the Million

There are about twice as many bicycles as cars in the world today – more than 800 million! In China alone there are probably over 100 million bicycles.

Did you know?

The world's largest bicycle, built in California, has wheels with a diameter of 10 feet and a circumference of nearly $31\frac{1}{2}$ feet.

Super Cycle

Modern racing bikes are lightweight and streamlined to "cut" through the air. This super cycle weighs only 11 pounds. The fastest speed a cyclist has reached is about 55 miles per hour.

REAR WHEEL
Diameter:
27 inches

Circumference:
approximately 85 inches

FRONT WHEEL
Diameter:
$3\frac{1}{2}$ inches

Circumference:
approximately
14 inches

ACROSS AND AROUND

Wheels and other circular objects are made in many different sizes. However, no matter how much circumferences and diameters vary, the relationship between these two measurements is always the same.

Parts of a Circle

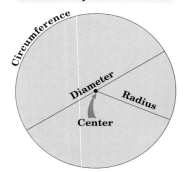

Comparing Circumference and Diameter

You will need:
- a colored streamer, ribbon, or string
- a large circular object (For example, you could use a table, bicycle wheel, or laundry basket.)

STEP 1: Circle and cut

Carefully place the streamer around the circumference of the circular object. Mark and cut the streamer so that it is the same length as the circumference.

STEP 2: How many diameters?

Extend the streamer across the diameter of the circular object. Estimate how many times the diameter would fit along the length of the circumference.

- Write about what you discovered.

1. Follow the steps on page 16 to compare the circumference and diameter of a variety of circular objects.

Look at the chart below.

2. Compare the data for Circles A and B. What do you notice about:

   a. the circumferences?
   b. the diameters?
   c. the circumference divided by the diameter?

3. a. Use a calculator to check the figure in the last column for Circle A.

   b. Copy and complete the chart, using your calculator to help. Write each answer so that it is correct to two decimal places. What did you notice?

4. Make a chart such as the one below for the bicycle wheels described on pages 14 and 15.

Circle	Circumference	Diameter	Circumference divided by diameter
A	22 inches	7 inches	3.14
B	44 inches	14 inches	3.14
C	88 inches	28 inches	
D	176 inches	56 inches	
E	352 inches	112 inches	

The official name
The relationship between a circle's circumference and its diameter has been known for thousands of years. In 1706, Englishman William Jones suggested that the exact value of "circumference divided by diameter" should be called *pi* (π), a letter of the Greek alphabet. The name *pi* and the symbol π are still used today.

Ups and Downs

Ferris wheels and roller coasters are all about the "fun" of the ride – dangling in a carriage high above the ground, or zooming down steep descents and through all kinds of twists and turns.

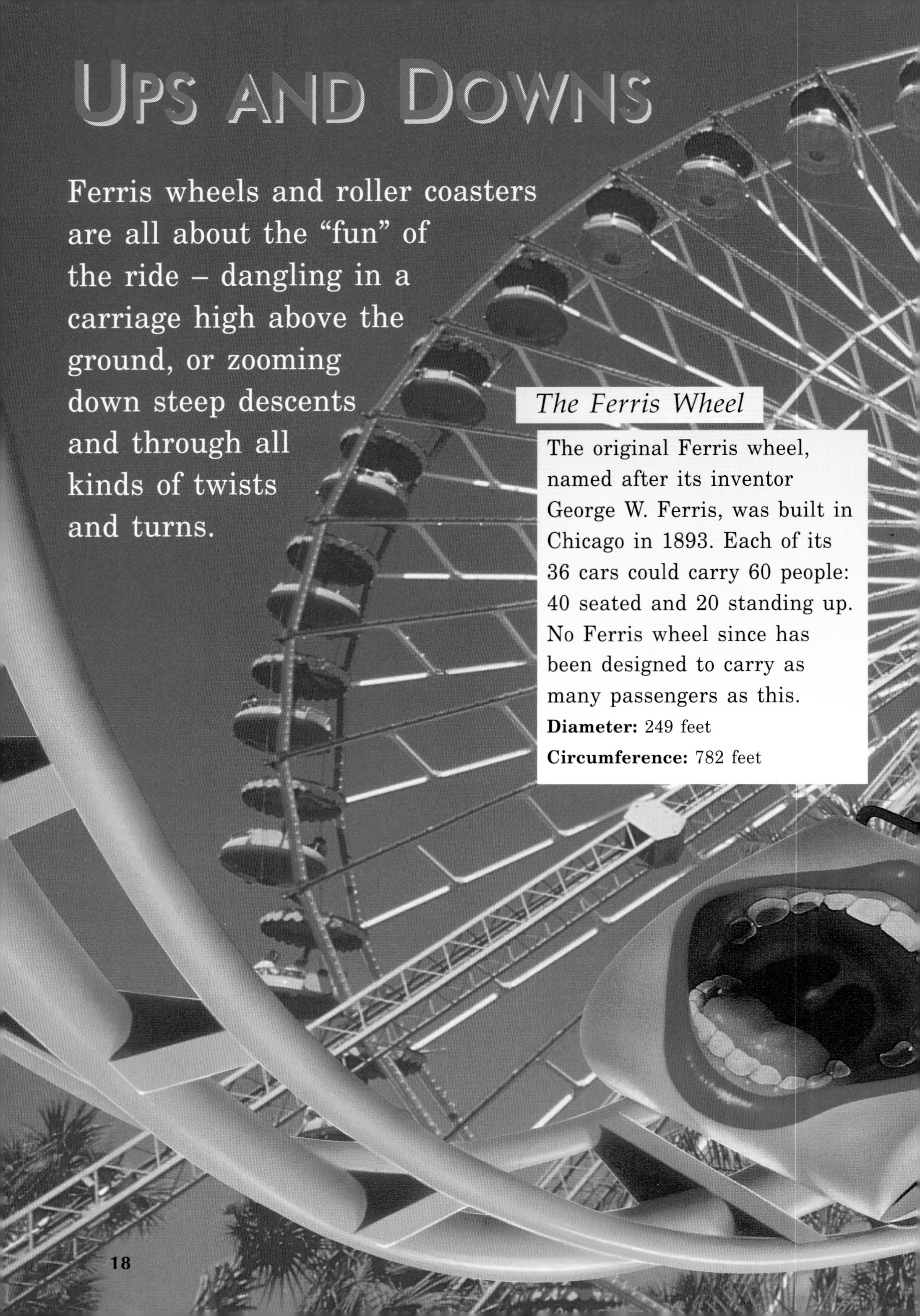

The Ferris Wheel

The original Ferris wheel, named after its inventor George W. Ferris, was built in Chicago in 1893. Each of its 36 cars could carry 60 people: 40 seated and 20 standing up. No Ferris wheel since has been designed to carry as many passengers as this.

Diameter: 249 feet

Circumference: 782 feet

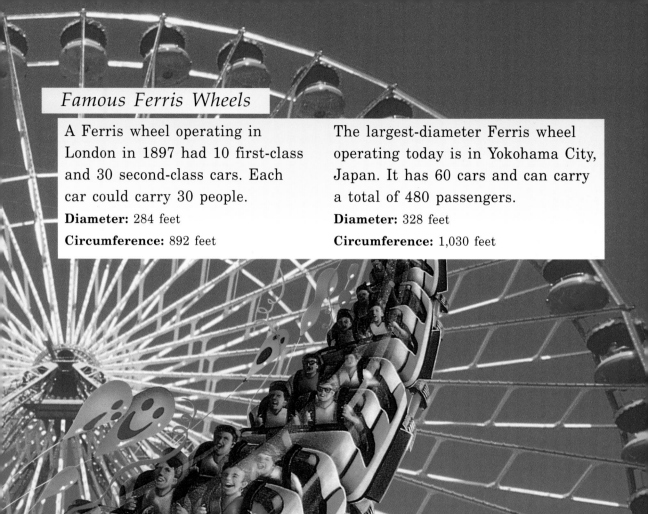

Famous Ferris Wheels

A Ferris wheel operating in London in 1897 had 10 first-class and 30 second-class cars. Each car could carry 30 people.

Diameter: 284 feet

Circumference: 892 feet

The largest-diameter Ferris wheel operating today is in Yokohama City, Japan. It has 60 cars and can carry a total of 480 passengers.

Diameter: 328 feet

Circumference: 1,030 feet

Roller Coaster Racers

Roller coasters carry their passengers at speeds of up to 85 miles per hour. Usually the whole ride lasts just a few minutes. The world's longest roller coaster, in England, takes passengers on a ride that lasts 5 minutes and 53 seconds, and covers 2,503 yards of track. Two trains can take 800 people each hour.

HIGHS AND LOWS

There is a slow climb to the top of the first hill on a roller coaster ride. But what goes up must come down – and on a roller coaster you come down *very* fast!

Facts and Figures for Three Roller Coasters

NAME	LOCATION	PASSENGERS PER CAR	CARS PER TRAIN	RIDE TIME
Desperado	Nevada, U.S.A.	6	5	2 min. 43 sec.
Le Monstre	Quebec, Canada	4	7	2 min. 30 sec.
Magnum XL-200	Ohio, U.S.A.	6	6	2 min. 0 sec.

Heights and Drops

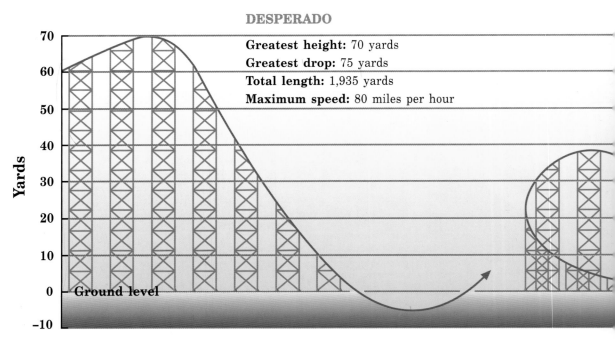

DESPERADO

Greatest height: 70 yards
Greatest drop: 75 yards
Total length: 1,935 yards
Maximum speed: 80 miles per hour

1. Compare the heights of the three roller coasters. What did you find out?
2. How far below ground level would you go on Desperado?
3. How many passengers can travel in one train on each roller coaster?
4. Estimate the number of rides that could take place on each roller coaster in one hour. Allow time for loading and unloading.
5. How many passengers could ride on each roller coaster in one hour?
6. Look at the information about Ferris wheels on pages 18 and 19. Compare:
   a. the sizes of the Ferris wheels
   b. the number of passengers each Ferris wheel could carry.

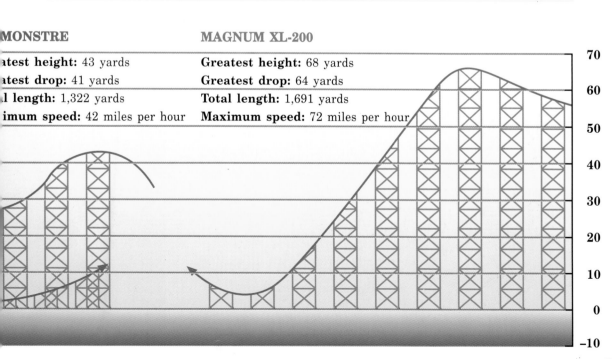

MONSTRE

atest height: 43 yards
atest drop: 41 yards
l length: 1,322 yards
imum speed: 42 miles per hour

MAGNUM XL-200

Greatest height: 68 yards
Greatest drop: 64 yards
Total length: 1,691 yards
Maximum speed: 72 miles per hour

CARRYING CARGO

Goods of all kinds are sent from place to place every day, often from one side of the world to the other. Trucks, trains, and planes are all used to keep this cargo on the move; however, most *international* cargo is carried by ships.

In the Air

Some planes, like this 747 freighter, carry only cargo. Cargo is also carried in special "holds" in most passenger planes. Cargo containers are specially designed to fit the space available in planes.

Did you know?

The largest container ships can carry more than 4,000 standard 20-foot containers. There are also huge ships, known as "supertankers," which carry oil. These measure up to 1,500 feet in length and hold more than 3 million barrels of oil. (One barrel is 42 gallons.)

Still Shipping

About 92 percent of the world's cargo is transported by sea. Sending cargo by air is faster, but is usually much more expensive.

A Perfect Fit

Since the late 1960s, containers used for sea *and* land transport have been made in two standard sizes. One is 20 feet long, 8 feet wide, and $8\frac{1}{2}$ feet high. The other is the same width and height, but double the length. All countries measure shipping containers in feet, even if they usually use metric measurements.

PACK IT IN !

Sending cargo can be very expensive, so people cannot afford to waste space. Careful packing and standard-sized containers help to make the best possible use of the space that is available.

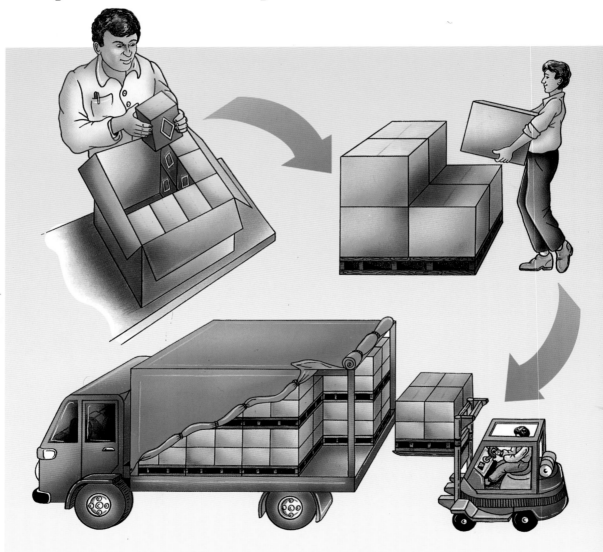

How many of the boxes with the diamond design could be packed into *two* trucks?

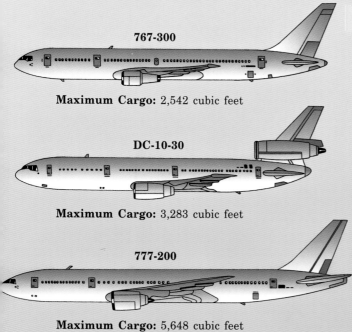

767-300

Maximum Cargo: 2,542 cubic feet

DC-10-30

Maximum Cargo: 3,283 cubic feet

777-200

Maximum Cargo: 5,648 cubic feet

Some Air-Cargo Containers

Container	Volume
A	212 cubic feet
B	141 cubic feet
C	353 cubic feet

All these planes can carry the containers listed in the chart. A plane could be packed with just one type of container or with combinations of two or three types.

1. Answer the question on page 24. Show the steps you use.

2. Look at the data at the top of this page. How many type-B containers could each plane carry?

3. Suppose you had 847 cubic feet of cargo to transport. What are some different combinations of containers you could use?

4. Suppose you had cargo filling 4 type-A containers, 4 type-B containers, and 6 type-C containers. What is the smallest plane that could carry all the containers?

5. What combinations of the three types of containers might be used in the 777?

6. Suppose you were designing a container with a volume of 360 cubic feet. What are some possible dimensions you could use?

COMING AND GOING

Some international airports are like small cities. The world's busiest airport (O'Hare airport in Chicago) covers nearly 7,700 acres and serves more than 66 million passengers each year.

Part of Chicago's O'Hare airport photographed from the air.

Passengers are given a boarding pass that shows their seat number and flight details.

Tokyo International Airport

Airport Traffic for One Year

This chart shows the annual traffic at a range of airports around the world.

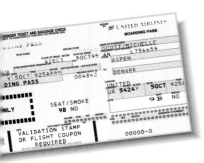

Airport	Aircraft Arriving and Departing (in thousands)	Passengers Arriving and Departing (in thousands)
Auckland	113	6,539
Chicago (O'Hare)	883	66,468
Denver	531	33,133
Frankfurt	365	35,123
Hong Kong	162	25,949
London (Heathrow)	425	51,718
Los Angeles	690	51,050
Miami	558	30,203
San Francisco	422	34,643
Sydney	263	19,076

CHECKING IN

For safety reasons, airlines place limits on the amount of baggage a plane may carry. Each class of passenger has a different baggage allowance.

Check In

Baggage that is to go in the aircraft's "hold" is weighed as passengers check in. This allows the total weight of "checked" baggage to be calculated for each plane.

BAGGAGE ALLOWANCES (per passenger)

1. CABIN BAGGAGE
Any combination of the following baggage is allowed on board.
a. One *Briefcase* or One *Small Bag*, not exceeding:
Depth 9 inches   Height 13 inches   Length 19 inches

PLUS

One *Garment Bag*, not exceeding (unfolded):
Thickness 4 inches   Width 24 inches   Length 45 inches

OR

b. Two *Briefcases* or Two *Small Bags*, each not exceeding:
Depth 9 inches   Height 13 inches   Length 19 inches

2. CHECKED BAGGAGE
In addition to cabin baggage, passengers are entitled to the following free baggage allowance, provided the *total dimensions* (*i.e. Depth plus Height plus Length*) of each item do not exceed 62 inches.

First Class	88 lb
Business Class	66 lb
Coach Class	44 lb
Infants (Not Occupying Seat)	22 lb

Passengers whose bags do not fit these specifications will be required to pay an excess baggage charge.

How Much to Take?

This card shows one airline's baggage allowances.

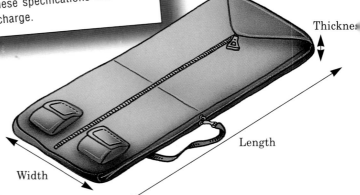
Garment Bag (Unfolded)

Thickness

Length

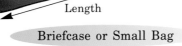
Briefcase or Small Bag

Height

Depth   Length

Width

Look at the baggage allowances shown on page 28.

1. Suppose a passenger had two items of cabin baggage. List all the possible combinations that he or she could carry on board.

2. Which of the following bags could be taken on board as cabin baggage?

Garment Bag (Folded)

Briefcase

Small Bag

14 in.

24 in.

n.

8 in.

18 in.

6 in.

22 in.

8 in.

22 in.

3. Which of these bags could be checked by a coach-class passenger without an excess baggage charge?

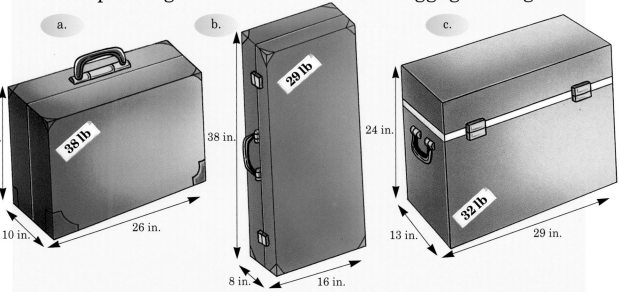

a.

b.

c.

29 lb

38 lb

38 in.

24 in.

32 lb

10 in.

26 in.

8 in.

16 in.

13 in.

29 in.

4. Suppose you are a business-class passenger. Describe the largest possible items of baggage you could check onto your flight. List several possibilities.

ALONG THE LINE

In 1913, Henry Ford became the first car maker to use an *assembly line* in his factory. Conveyor belts moved parts along, and each worker had a special task that was repeated on each car. Many modern vehicle assembly lines use robots.

The picture graph shows how many vehicles are made by the top five car-producing countries in an average year. The populations of these countries are shown below the graph.

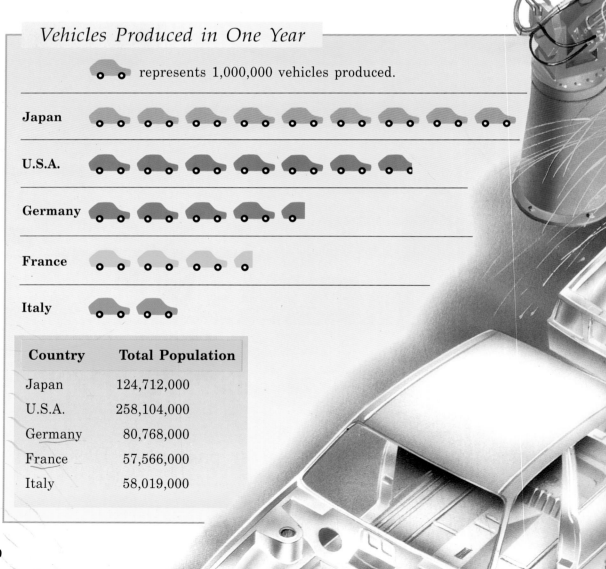

Vehicles Produced in One Year

🚗 represents 1,000,000 vehicles produced.

Country	Total Population
Japan	124,712,000
U.S.A.	258,104,000
Germany	80,768,000
France	57,566,000
Italy	58,019,000

Fast Fords

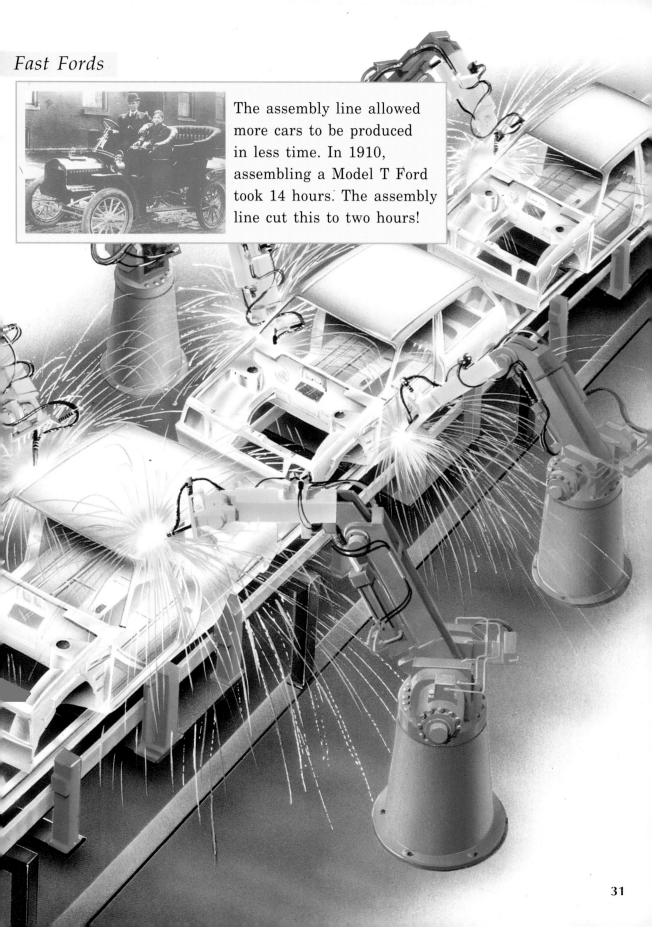

The assembly line allowed more cars to be produced in less time. In 1910, assembling a Model T Ford took 14 hours. The assembly line cut this to two hours!

BRIGHT AND SHINY

In 1913, all the cars rolling off Henry Ford's assembly line were black. Today's car factories produce cars in a variety of colors – usually with different quantities of each color.

The pie graphs show the percentages of different-colored cars produced at four car factories. This chart shows how many cars the factories produce each week.

Cars Produced Per Week	
Factories	**Cars**
Branford	3,000
Hayward	8,000
Montville	6,000
Westly	7,000

Which Color?

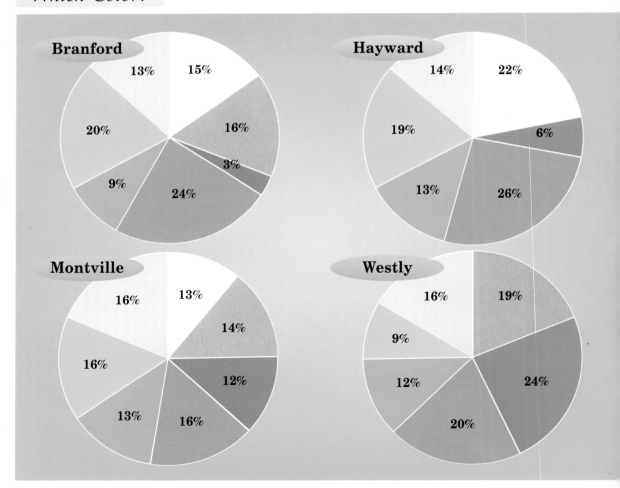

A car having its paint "baked" on.

1. Which factory produces about twice as many yellow cars as green cars?
2. Which factory comes closest to producing the same percentage of cars in each color?
3. How many cars at each factory are likely to be yellow:
   a. out of every 100 cars produced?
   b. out of every 1,000 cars produced?
4. Suppose each factory produces 10,000 cars. How many in each factory are likely to be green?
5. Look at the chart showing numbers of cars produced. How many white cars are likely to be produced in one week at:
   a. Branford?   b. Montville?

SAIL AWAY

Sailing ships have carried people and goods across oceans and seas for thousands of years. Some of today's largest ships still use sails at times.

Endeavour   Built 1760

Captain Cook sailed in the small three-masted ship, *Endeavour*, on his voyage of discovery from England to the east coast of Australia. The journey took almost three years, from 1768 to 1771.

Passengers and crew: 94

Length: 101 feet 7 inches

Width: 28 feet 7 inches

Weight: 370 tons

1. Foremast
2. Anchor
3. Main deck
4. Main hatch
5. Mainmast
6. Officers' deck
7. Wheel
8. Rear mast
9. Great cabin
10. Botanist's cabin
11. Astronomer's cabin
12. Captain Cook's cabin
13. Galley
14. Sail room
15. Ship's supplies
16. Steward's room
17. Surgeon's cabin

Great Eastern   Built 1858

This British liner was twice as long and five times as heavy as any other ship of its time. In addition to its sails, it had a four-bladed propeller and two paddle wheels.

Passengers and crew: 2,996

Length: 688 feet 6 inches

Width: 83 feet

Weight: 18,915 tons

Club Med 2   Built 1990

This modern sail-assisted cruise liner is the longest sailing ship in the world. When there is not enough wind, a computer automatically switches the ship to propeller power.

Passengers and crew: 586

Length: 613 feet 2 inches

Width: 65 feet 6 inches

Weight: 16,253 tons

WATERWAYS

For hundreds of years, explorers tried to find waterways that would shorten sea journeys. Finally, two major canals were constructed to cut through land bridges between continents. By avoiding the Cape of Good Hope and Cape Horn, sea captains were able to travel more safely and save time and money.

Suez Canal

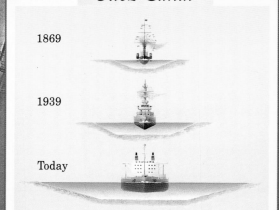

1869

1939

Today

The Suez Canal links the Red Sea to the Mediterranean Sea. When it was opened in 1869, it was only $26\frac{1}{2}$ feet deep and 231 feet wide. Since then it has been widened several times, so that most large ships can pass through.

Length: 114 miles

Depth: 63 feet

Width at surface: 746 feet

Panama Canal

The Panama Canal, which links the Pacific Ocean to the Atlantic Ocean, opened in 1914. It took 10 years to build. On average, 33 ships pass through it every day, making it the busiest canal in the world.

Length: $48\frac{1}{2}$ miles

Depth: 43 feet (minimum)

Width at surface: 495 feet (at narrowest point)

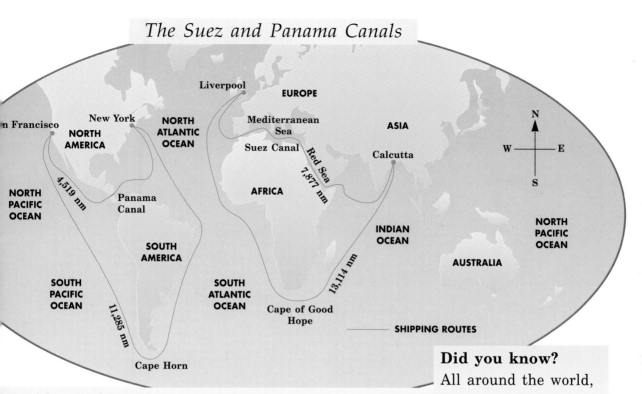

The Suez and Panama Canals

Map labels:
Liverpool, EUROPE, New York, NORTH ATLANTIC OCEAN, n Francisco, NORTH AMERICA, Mediterranean Sea, Suez Canal, ASIA, NORTH PACIFIC OCEAN, Red Sea 7,877 nm, Calcutta, AFRICA, 4,519 nm, Panama Canal, NORTH PACIFIC OCEAN, NORTH PACIFIC OCEAN, INDIAN OCEAN, SOUTH AMERICA, AUSTRALIA, SOUTH PACIFIC OCEAN, SOUTH ATLANTIC OCEAN, 13,114 nm, 11,285 nm, Cape of Good Hope, Cape Horn, SHIPPING ROUTES

Compass: N, W, E, S

Did you know?
All around the world, distances across water are measured in *nautical miles* (nm). A nautical mile is equal to 1.112 miles.

1. About how many ships pass through the Panama Canal each year?
2. Suppose a ship had to travel from San Francisco to New York. How many nautical miles would be saved by using the Panama Canal?
3. How many nautical miles would be saved by using the Suez Canal to sail between Calcutta and Liverpool?
4. Suppose that a ship traveled at an average of 20 nautical miles per hour. How many days would it take to travel each route between:
   a. San Francisco and New York?
   b. Calcutta and Liverpool?

Research
• The Panama Canal uses water chambers called *locks*. Find out how locks work.

200 YEARS ON THE MOV

LAND

1870 (U.K.)
The first "penny-farth
bicycle was made.

1804 (U.K.)
English engineer
Richard Trevithick
invented the first
successful steam-
powered locomotive.

1830 (U.K.)
The first regular steam
locomotive passenger service
opened. It ran between
Liverpool and Manchester.

1863 (U.K.)
The world's
first
underground
railway
opened in
London.

SEA

1838 (U.K.)
The *Sirius* offered the
first regular steamship
service across the
Atlantic Ocean,
from Liverpool to
New York.

1807 (U.S.A.)
American Robert
Fulton built the first
successful steamboat.

1858 (U.K.)
The British launched
the *Great Eastern*, the
largest ship the world
had ever seen.

AIR

1852 (France)
French inventor Henri
Giffard launched the
world's first successful
airship, a balloon
powered by a steam
engine. Modern hot-air
balloons are popular for
leisure flights.

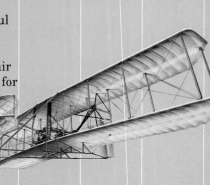

1990 (France)
The French
T.G.V. train
recorded the
fastest speed
for a passenger
train, reaching
320 miles per
hour.

1913 (U.S.A.)
American Henry
Ford developed an
assembly line to
mass-produce his
Model T Fords.

1937 (Germany)
Mass production of the
Volkswagen "Beetle"
started in Germany.
The Beetle is the most
popular car ever made.

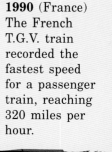

1959 (U.K.)
Christopher Cockerell
designed and built the first
hovercraft. Cushioned by
compressed air, hovercrafts
can travel on land *or* sea.

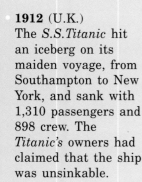

1912 (U.K.)
The *S.S.Titanic* hit
an iceberg on its
maiden voyage, from
Southampton to New
York, and sank with
1,310 passengers and
898 crew. The
Titanic's owners had
claimed that the ship
was unsinkable.

1990 (France)
Launch of
the longest
sailing ship in
the world, the
Club Med 2.
It measures
558 feet in
length.

1981 (U.S.A.)
Launch of the first
space shuttle.

1996 (U.S.A.)
The 777
Stretch, the
world's longest
passenger
plane, made
its first
commercial
flight.

03 (U.S.A.)
ville and Wilbur
right's *Flyer* took
the skies for
der a minute,
coming the first
rplane to fly.

1970 (U.S.A.)
The Boeing 747
jumbo jet began
service. It could
carry hundreds
of passengers and
made international
air travel more
affordable.

1976 (U.S.A.)
The Concorde, the
world's fastest
plane, started
service between
Europe and the
U.S.A. A Concorde's
cruising speed is
1,354 miles per hour.

39

GLOSSARY

Average
A number that is used to represent a set of numbers. Averages can be calculated in different ways. The average that is known as the *mean* is calculated by dividing the **total** of the values in a set by the **number** of values in a set.

Circumference
The line that forms a circle, or the length of that line.

Diameter
A line across a circle or sphere that passes through the center and connects two points on the circumference. The distance represented by this line is also called the diameter.

Percent/Percentage
Percent means "out of, or divided by, one hundred."

For example, 34 percent means 34 divided by 100, and or $\frac{34}{100}$. When you have 100 percent of something ($\frac{100}{100}$), it means that you have the total amount; if you have 50 percent, you have $\frac{50}{100}$ or one half of the total. The symbol % is often used to indicate percentage.

Pi (π)
The ratio of the circumference of a circle to its diameter. This ratio is the same for every circle. Its value, which is found by dividing the circumference by the diameter, is a little more than 3.14.

Pie graph
A circle marked into sectors. Each sector shows the fraction represented by one category of data.

Radius
A line from any point on the edge of a circle or sphere to its center. The distance represented by this line is also called the radius.

Ratio
A comparison of two numbers. For example, i three people had black hair and two people had brown hair, the ratio of black to brown would be "3 to 2"; this could be written as 3:2. Ratio car also be thought about in terms of division; for example, 3:2 could be thought of as 3÷2, or $\frac{3}{2}$.

Volume
The amount of space inside a 3-dimensional shape or occupied by a solid. Volume is measured in *cubic* units, such as a cubic foot.

INDEX